INSIGHTS
Easter

INSIGHTS
Easter

What the Bible Tells Us about the Easter Story

WILLIAM BARCLAY

SAINT ANDREW PRESS
Edinburgh

First published in 2008 by
SAINT ANDREW PRESS
121 George Street
Edinburgh EH2 4YN

ISBN 978 0 7152 0860 1

British Library Cataloguing in Publication Data
A catalogue record for this book is available from the British Library

It is the Publisher's policy to only use papers that are natural and
recyclable and that have been manufactured from timber grown in
renewable, properly managed forests. All of the manufacturing
processes of the papers are expected to conform to the environmental
regulations of the country of origin.

Typeset by Waverley Typesetters, Fakenham
Printed and bound by Bell & Bain Ltd, Glasgow

Contents

Foreword

At last! I've discovered William Barclay, the Christian's best kept secret (at least to this generation!) and he's brilliant. I would describe his commentaries as the theological *Brodie's Notes* I've been searching for and didn't know exist. Thanks to Barclay I'm now devouring my Bible in the same insatiable way some devour a bestselling novel. The Bible is brimming with texture and dimension and history and politics and romance and heartache and promise and love and more and at last it is coming into full focus for me.

My new-found Bible-reading experience reminds me of the satisfaction I used to have as a professional actress during rehearsals. The process of transforming the words on the page of my script into a believable, living, breathing character, thrilled me. I revelled in the creative collaboration between actor and director as we strove to get to the heart of the play. Ultimately though, it was the director's responsibility to have an overview, to capture the meaning of the play – in short, to tell the story.

It can be argued that, similarly, the *Insights* series takes on the role of director in breaking with tradition to examine the Easter story. Even though this method, like that of any other serious Bible commentary, involves extensive, critical examination and interpretation of the text, it opts out of following the conventional verse-by-verse structure. Instead, it examines the Easter story by leap-frogging around scripture 'for the sake of keeping the narrative continuous'.

At first glance, this approach may seem chaotic, but it soon becomes evident that looking at the story from different 'camera angles' (whether it be form one of the gospels, or Acts or Corinthians) enhances the intensity of the story. The insight gained by galvanising the narrative tool transforms our understanding.

In my opinion, the decision to use this device is a stroke of genius as it allows the commentary to go beyond the boundaries of a typical exegesis. It frees Barclay up to engage with the reader and, like any great director, to stay committed to telling the story.

Barclay teaches, probes, advices, and disturbs. In fact, as we use these notes to aid our Bible-reading experience, we cannot help but be personally challenged. We are compelled into a dialogue. He doesn't allow us the luxury of a passive read. The experience is much more dynamic than that.

Driven by his passion for God, he's committed to sharing his great wealth of knowledge with the rest of us in a language that is intelligent, straightforward and free from confusing jargon. He has the gift of making the almost inexplicably complex, clear.

And Barclay isn't afraid of exposing his heart. His under-lying agenda is obvious.

Barclay is passionate for us to know God and by knowing Him to be significantly changed, transformed. Barclay encourages us to do so through understanding more of Jesus. Thanks to his direction we get a stronger sense of the multi-faceted magnificence of Jesus. For me Barclay really strikes a chord when he highlights Jesus' capacity to forgive, above anything else.

'Jesus said many wonderful things, but rarely anything more wonderful than, "Father, forgive them, for they know not what they do." Christian forgiveness is an amazing thing … There is nothing so lovely and nothing so rare as Christian forgiveness.'

Without doubt Barclay is an exciting bold mix of heart and mind. Jesus said the greatest of all the commandments is to love God with *all* our heart, mind, soul and strength. In Barclay we see a man who takes that commandment seriously.

Barclay is essential reading. He was way ahead of his time and is still utterly contemporary. There couldn't be a better time to read everything he's written and I recommend beginning with the *Insights* series – you won't be disappointed.

DIANE LOUISE JORDAN

Introduction

Most of us know the basics of the Easter story, but the details and the characters of this drama are surprising.

Jesus arrived in Jerusalem on a donkey which, as we all know, showed that he came meek and lowly. Yet in those days, as William Barclay points out, 'when a king went to war he rode on a horse, when he came in peace he rode on a donkey.' In one simple gesture, Jesus upset the expectations of the people, who were hoping for a warrior king, yet he also struck fear into the hearts of the ruling establishment, who saw him arriving as a king. Insights such as these turn the familiar story into something much more challenging and revealing.

In the Bible, each of the four gospels has its own description of events. In *Insights: Easter*, we have selected passages from each – and from the Acts of the Apostles and the First Letter to the Corinthians – to create a gripping account of a tense drama played out by a cast of fascinating characters. Pontius Pilate has to play his cards carefully in a dangerous political game, with his Roman masters on one side and the Jewish authorities on the other. Judas, who betrays Jesus, can be seen as either evil personified or as deserving our understanding. Why was Joseph from Arimathea called the 'secret disciple'? Who were the Sanhedrin, and why were they so against Jesus? Was Thomas's doubt a sign of weakness or strength? Who was the mysterious young man who appears in Mark's gospel, but in none of the other gospels, on the night of Jesus' arrest?

William Barclay offers explanations for all of these and more in *Insights: Easter*. Each story is animated with anecdotes and enlightening comments, all written to help us to understand the Bible in new ways. There is, of course, insufficient room in this book to cover Barclay's full commentary on each gospel's version. If you want to read more about the Easter stories, you can find them in Barclay's New Daily Study Bible series, in the following volumes: Matthew vol. 2, Mark, Luke and John vol. 2. Barclay's full commentary on the Acts of the Apostles describes what happened to the early church. These are all available from Saint Andrew Press.

The coming of the King

Mark 11:1–6

When they were coming near to Jerusalem, to Bethphage and to Bethany, Jesus despatched two of his disciples, and said to them, 'Go into the village opposite you, and as soon as you come into it, you will find tethered there a colt, on which no man has ever yet sat. Loose it and bring it to me. And if anyone says to you, "Why are you doing this?" say, "The Lord needs it," and immediately he will send it.' And they went away and they found the colt tethered, outside a door, on the open street, and they loosed it. And some of those who were standing by said to them, 'What are you doing loosing this colt?' They said to them what Jesus had told them to say, and they let them go.

We have come to the last stage of the journey. There had been the time of withdrawal around Caesarea Philippi in the far north. There had been the time in Galilee. There had been the stay in the hill country of Judaea and in the regions beyond Jordan. There had been the road through Jericho. Now comes Jerusalem.

We have to note something without which the story is almost unintelligible. When we read the first three gospels we get the idea that this was actually Jesus' first visit to Jerusalem.

They are concerned to tell the story of Jesus' work in Galilee. We must remember that the gospels are very short. Into their short compass is crammed the work of three years, and the writers were bound to select the things in which they were interested and of which they had special knowledge. And when we read the Fourth Gospel we find Jesus frequently in Jerusalem (John 2:13, 5:1, 7:10). We find in fact that he regularly went up to Jerusalem for the great feasts.

There is no real contradiction here. The first three gospels are specially interested in the Galilaean ministry, and the fourth in the Judaean. In fact, moreover, even the first three have indications that Jesus was not infrequently in Jerusalem. There is his close friendship with Martha and Mary and Lazarus at Bethany, a friendship which speaks of many visits. There is the fact that Joseph of Arimathaea was his secret friend. And above all there is Jesus' saying in Matthew 23:37 that often he would have gathered together the people of Jerusalem as a hen gathers her chickens under her wings but they were unwilling. Jesus could not have said that unless there had previously been more than one appeal which had met with a cold response.

This explains the incident of the colt. Jesus did not leave things until the last moment. He knew what he was going to do and long ago he had made arrangements with a friend. When he sent forward his disciples, he sent them with a password that had been prearranged – 'The Lord needs it now.' This was not a sudden, reckless decision of Jesus. It was something to which all his life had been building up.

Bethphage and Bethany were villages near Jerusalem. Very probably *Bethphage* means *house of figs* and *Bethany* means *house of dates*. They must have been very close because we know from the Jewish law that Bethphage was one of the circle of villages which marked the limit of a Sabbath day's journey, that is, less than a mile, while Bethany was one of the recognized lodging places for pilgrims to the Passover when Jerusalem was full.

The prophets of Israel had always had a very distinctive method of getting their message across. When words failed to move people they did something dramatic, as if to say, 'If you will not hear, you must be compelled to see' (cf. specially 1 Kings 11:30–2). These dramatic actions were what we might call acted warnings or dramatic sermons. That method was what Jesus was employing here. His action was a deliberate dramatic claim to be the Messiah.

But we must be careful to note just what he was doing. There was a saying of the prophet Zechariah (Zechariah 9:9), 'Rejoice greatly, O daughter Zion! Shout aloud, O daughter Jerusalem! Lo, your king comes to you; triumphant and victorious is he, humble and riding on a donkey, on a colt, the foal of a donkey.' The whole impact is that *the King was coming in peace*. In Palestine the donkey was not a despised animal, but a noble one. When a king went to war he rode on a horse, when he came in peace he rode on a donkey.

Nowadays the donkey is an animal of amused contempt, but in the time of Jesus it was the animal used to bear kings. But we must note *what kind of a king Jesus was claiming to be*. He came meek and lowly. He came in peace and for peace. They greeted him as the Son of David, but they did not understand.

It was just at this time that the Hebrew poems, The Psalms of Solomon, were written. They represent the kind of Son

of David whom people expected. Here is their description
of him:

> Behold, O Lord, and raise up unto them their king, the son
>   of David,
>> At the time, in which thou seest, O God, that he may
>> reign over Israel, thy servant.
> And gird him with strength that he may shatter unrighteous
>   rulers,
>> And that he may purge Jerusalem from nations that
>> trample her down to destruction.
> Wisely, righteously he shall thrust out sinners from the
>   inheritance,
>> He shall destroy the pride of sinners as a potter's
>> vessel.
> With a rod of iron he shall break in pieces all their substance.
>> He shall destroy the godless nations with the word of
>> his mouth.
> At his rebuke nations shall flee before him,
>> And he shall reprove sinners for the thoughts of their
>> hearts.
>
> · · ·
>
> All nations shall be in fear before him,
> For he will smite the earth with the word of his mouth
>   forever.
>
>   (Psalms of Solomon 17:21–5, 39)

That was the kind of poem on which the people nourished
their hearts. They were looking for a king who would shatter
and smash and break. Jesus knew it – and he came meek and
lowly, riding upon a donkey.

When Jesus rode into Jerusalem that day, he claimed to be king, but he claimed to be King of peace. His action was a contradiction of everything that was hoped for and expected.

⟨⟩

The last meal together

Luke 22:7–23

There came the day of the Feast of Unleavened Bread, on which the Passover had to be sacrificed. Jesus despatched Peter and John. 'Go,' he said, 'and make ready the Passover for us that we may eat it.' They said to him, 'Where do you want us to make it ready?' 'Look you,' he said to them, 'when you have gone into the city, a man will meet you, carrying a jar of water. Follow him to the house into which he enters; and you will say to the master of the house, "The Teacher says to you, 'Where is the guest room that I may eat the Passover with my disciples?'" And he will show you a big upper room, ready furnished. There, get things ready.' So they went away and found everything just as he had told them; and they made ready the Passover.

When the hour came he took his place at table, and so did his disciples. 'I have desired with all my heart', he said to them, 'to eat this Passover with you before I suffer, for I tell you that I will not eat it until it is fulfilled in the kingdom of God.' He received the cup, and gave thanks, and said, 'Take this and divide it among yourselves.

For I tell you that from now on I will not drink of the fruit of the vine until the kingdom of God has come.' And he took the bread, and gave thanks, and broke it, and gave it to them, saying, 'This is my body which is being given for you. Do this so that you will remember me.' In the same way, after the meal, he took the cup saying, 'This cup is the new covenant made at the price of my blood, which is shed for you. But – look you – the hand of him who betrays me is on the table with me, for the Son of Man goes as it has been determined. But woe to that man by whom he has been betrayed'; and they began to question one another which of them it could be who was going to do this.

ONCE again Jesus did not leave things until the last moment; his plans were already made. The better-class houses had two rooms. The one room was on the top of the other; and the house looked exactly like a small box placed on top of a large one. The upper room was reached by an outside stair. During the Passover time all lodging in Jerusalem was free. The only pay a host might receive for letting lodgings to the pilgrims was the skin of the lamb which was eaten at the feast. A very usual use of an upper room was that it was the place where a Rabbi met with his favourite disciples to talk things over with them and to open his heart to them. Jesus had taken steps to procure such a room. He sent Peter and John into the city to look for a man bearing a jar of water. To carry water was a woman's task. A man carrying a jar of water would have been very easy to pick out. This was a prearranged signal between Jesus and a friend.

So the feast went on; and Jesus used the ancient symbols and gave them a new meaning.

(1) He said of the bread, 'This is my body.' Herein is exactly what we mean by a sacrament. A sacrament is something, usually a very ordinary thing, which has acquired a meaning far beyond itself for those who have eyes to see and hearts to understand. There is nothing specially theological or mysterious about this.

In the house of every one of us there is a drawer full of things which can only be called junk, and yet we will not throw them out, because when we touch and handle and look at them, they bring back this or that person, or this or that occasion. They are common things but they have a meaning far beyond themselves. That is a sacrament.

When the mother of the writer J. M. Barrie died and her belongings were being cleared, it was discovered that she had kept all the envelopes in which her famous son had posted her the cheques he so faithfully and lovingly sent. They were only old envelopes but they meant much to her. That is a sacrament.

When Nelson was buried in St Paul's Cathedral a party of his sailors bore his coffin to the tomb. One who saw the scene wrote, 'With reverence and with efficiency they lowered the body of the world's greatest admiral into its tomb. Then, as though answering to a sharp order from the quarterdeck, they all seized the Union Jack with which the coffin had been covered and tore it to fragments, and each took his souvenir of the illustrious dead.' All their lives that little bit of coloured cloth would speak to them of the admiral they had loved. That is a sacrament.

The bread which we eat at the sacrament is common bread, but, for anyone who has a heart to feel and understand, it is the very body of Christ.

(2) He said of the cup, 'This cup is the new covenant made at the price of my blood.' In the biblical sense, a covenant is a relationship between human beings and God. God graciously approached his people; and the people promised to obey and to keep his law. The whole matter is set out in Exodus 24:1–8. The continuance of that covenant depends on keeping that pledge and obeying this law; we could not and cannot do that; human sin interrupts our relationship with God. All the Jewish sacrificial system was designed to restore that relationship by the offering of sacrifice to God to atone for sin. What Jesus said was this – 'By my life and by my death I have made possible a new relationship between you and God. You are sinners. That is true. But because I died for you, God is no longer your enemy but your friend.' It cost the life of Christ to restore our lost relationship of friendship with God.

(3) Jesus said, 'Do this and it will make you remember me.' Jesus knew how easily the human mind forgets. The Greeks had an adjective which they used to describe time – 'time,' they said, 'which wipes all things out,' as if the human mind were a slate and time a sponge which wiped it clean. Jesus was saying, 'In the rush and press of things you will forget me. People forget because they must, and not because they want to. Come in sometimes to the peace and stillness of my house and do this again with my people – and you will remember.'

It made the tragedy all the more tragic that at that very table there was one who was a traitor. Jesus Christ has at every communion table those who betray him, for if in his house we pledge ourselves to turn and then by our lives go out to deny him, we too are traitors to him.

ᗝᐧ᜵

The Lord's Supper

1 Corinthians 11:23–34

For I received of the Lord that which I also handed on to you, that the Lord Jesus, on the night on which he was being delivered up, took bread, and, after he had given thanks, he broke it and said: 'This is my body which is for you; this do that you may remember me.' In the same way, after the meal, he took the cup and said: 'This cup is the new covenant and it cost my blood. Do this, as often as you drink it, so that you will remember me.' For as often as you eat this bread and drink this cup, you do proclaim the death of the Lord until he will come. Therefore whoever eats this bread and drinks this cup of the Lord in an unfitting way is guilty of a sin against the body and blood of the Lord. But let a man examine himself, and so let him eat of that bread and drink of that cup. For he who eats and drinks as some of you do, eats and drinks judgment to himself, because he does not discern what the body means. It is because of this that many among you are ill and weak and some have died. But, if we truly discerned what we are like, we would not be liable to judgment. But, in this very judgment of the Lord, we are being disciplined that we may not be finally condemned along with the world. So then, my brothers, when you come together, wait for each other. If anyone is hungry, let him eat at home, so that you may not meet together in such a way as to render yourselves liable to judgment. As for the other matters, I will put them in order when I shall have come.

No passage in the whole New Testament is of greater interest than this. For one thing, it gives us our warrant for the most sacred act of worship in the Church, the sacrament of the Lord's Supper; and, for another, since the letter to the Corinthians is earlier than the earliest of the gospels, this is actually the first recorded account we possess of any word of Jesus.

The sacrament can never mean the same for every person; but we do not need fully to understand it to benefit from it. As someone has said, 'We do not need to understand the chemistry of bread in order to digest it and to be nourished by it.' For all that, we do well to try at least to understand something of what Jesus meant when he spoke of the bread and the wine as he did.

'This is my body,' he said of the bread. One simple fact precludes us from taking this with a crude literalism. When Jesus spoke, he was still in the body; and there was nothing clearer than that his body and the bread were at that moment quite different things. Nor did he simply mean: 'This stands for my body.' In a sense, that is true. The broken bread of the sacrament does stand for the body of Christ; but it does more. To those who take it into their hands and upon their lips with faith and love, it is a means not only of memory but of living contact with Jesus Christ. To an unbeliever, it would be nothing; to all who love Christ, it is the way to his presence.

'This cup', said Jesus, in the usual version, 'is the new covenant in my blood.' We have translated it slightly differently: 'This cup is the new covenant and it cost my blood.' The Greek preposition *en* most commonly means *in*; but it can, and regularly does, mean *at the cost or price of*, especially when it translates the Hebrew preposition *be*. Now, a covenant is a relationship entered into between two people. There was an old covenant between God and his people, and that old relationship was based on *law*. In it, God chose and approached the people of Israel and became in a special sense their God; but there was a condition that, if this relationship was going to last, they must keep his law (cf. Exodus 24:1–8). With Jesus, a new relationship is opened to men and women, dependent not on law but on love, dependent not on their ability to keep the law – for no one can do that – but on the free grace of God's love offered to all.

Under the old covenant, people could do nothing other than fear God, for they were forever in default since they could never perfectly keep the law; under the new covenant, they come to God as children to a father. However you look at things, *it cost the life of Jesus to make this new relationship possible*. 'The blood is the life,' says the law (Deuteronomy 12:23); it cost Jesus' life, his blood, as the Jews would put it. And so the scarlet wine of the sacrament stands for the very lifeblood of Christ without which the new covenant, the new relationship of men and women to God, could never have been possible.

This passage goes on to talk about eating and drinking this bread and wine unworthily. The unworthiness consisted in the fact that those who did so did 'not discern the Lord's body'. That phrase can equally well mean two things, and each is so real and so important that it is quite likely that both are intended.

(1) It may mean that those who eat and drink unworthily do not realize what the sacred symbols mean. It may mean that they eat and drink with no reverence and no sense of the love that these symbols stand for, or the obligation that is laid upon them.

(2) It may also mean this. The phrase *the body of Christ* again and again stands for the Church. Paul has just been rebuking those who, with their divisions and their class distinctions, divide the Church; so, this may mean that the people who eat and drink unworthily are those who have never realized that the whole Church is the body of Christ but are at variance with others. All who hold in their hearts feelings of hatred, bitterness and contempt against others, as they come to the table of our Lord, eat and drink unworthily. So, to eat and drink unworthily is to do so with no sense of the greatness of the thing we do, and to do so while we are at variance with those others for whom also Christ died.

Paul goes on to say that the misfortunes which have fallen upon the church at Corinth may simply be due to the fact that they come to this sacrament while they are divided among themselves; but these misfortunes are sent not to destroy them but to discipline them and to bring them back to the right way.

We must be clear about one thing. The phrase which forbids people to eat and drink unworthily does not shut out the man or woman who is a sinner and knows it. An old highland minister, seeing an old woman hesitate to receive the cup, stretched it out to her, saying: 'Take it, woman; it's for sinners; it's for you.' If the table of Christ were only for perfect people, none might ever approach it. The way is never closed to the penitent sinner. To all who love God and their neighbours, the way is always open; and, as Isaiah had it, 'though your sins are like scarlet, they shall be like snow' (Isaiah 1:18).

Love's last appeal

Mark 14:17–21

> When it was evening, Jesus came with the Twelve. As they were reclining at table and eating, Jesus said, 'This is the truth I tell you – one of you will betray me, one who is eating with me.' They began to be grieved, and to say to him, one by one, 'Surely it cannot be I?' He said to them, 'One of the Twelve, one who dips his hand with me into the dish. The Son of Man goes as it stands written about him, but woe to that man through whom the Son of Man is betrayed. It had been good for him, if that man had not been born.'

THE new day began at 6 pm, and when the Passover evening had come, Jesus sat down with the Twelve. There was only one change in the old ritual which had been observed so many centuries ago in Egypt. At the first Passover Feast in Egypt, the meal had been eaten standing (Exodus 12:11). But that had been a sign of haste, a sign that they were slaves escaping from slavery. In the time of Jesus, the regulation was that the meal should be eaten reclining, for that was the sign of free people, with a home and a country of their own.

This is a poignant passage. All the time, there was a text running in Jesus' head. 'Even my bosom friend in whom I trusted, who ate of my bread, has lifted the heel against me' (Psalm 41:9). These words were in his mind all the time. We can see certain great things here.

(1) Jesus knew what was going to happen. That is his supreme courage, especially in the last days. It would have been easy for him to escape, and yet undeterred he went on. Homer relates how the great warrior Achilles was told that if he went out to his last battle he would surely be killed. His answer was, 'Nevertheless I am for going on.' With a full knowledge of what lay ahead, Jesus was for going on.

(2) Jesus could see into the heart of Judas. The curious thing is that the other disciples seem to have had no suspicions. If they had known what Judas was engaged on, it is certain that they would have stopped him even by violence. Here is something to remember. There may be things we succeed in hiding from other people, but we cannot hide them from Jesus Christ. He is the searcher of human hearts. He knows what is in each one of us. In J. G. Whittier's words:

> *Our thoughts lie open to thy sight;*
> *And naked to thy glance.*
> *Our secret sins are in the light*
> *Of thy pure countenance.*

Blessed indeed are the pure in heart.

(3) In this passage, we see Jesus offering two things to Judas.

(a) He is making love's last appeal. It is as if he is saying to Judas, 'I know what you are going to do. Will you not stop even now?'

(b) He is offering Judas a last warning. He is telling him in advance of the consequences of the thing that it is in his heart to do. But we must note this, for it is of the essence of the way in which God deals with us – *there is no compulsion*. Without a doubt, Jesus could have stopped Judas. All he had to do was tell the other eleven what Judas was planning, and Judas would never have left that room alive.

Here is the whole human situation. God has given us wills that are free. His love appeals to us. His truth warns us. But there is no compulsion. We hold the awful responsibility that we can spurn the appeal of God's love and disregard the warning of his voice. In the end, there is no one but ourselves responsible for our sins.

In Greek legend, two famous travellers passed the rocks where the Sirens sang. The Sirens sat on these rocks and sang with such sweetness that they lured mariners irresistibly to their doom. Ulysses sailed past these rocks. His method was to stop the sailors' ears so that they could not hear and order them to bind himself to the mast with ropes so that, however much he struggled, he would not be able to answer to that seductive sweetness. He resisted by compulsion. The other traveller was Orpheus, the sweetest musician of all. His method was to play and sing with such surpassing sweetness as his ship passed the rocks where the Sirens were, that the attraction of the song of the Sirens was never even felt because of the attraction of the song he sang. His method was to answer the appeal of seduction with a still greater appeal.

God's is the second way. He does not stop us, whether we like it or not, from sin. He seeks to make us love him so much that his voice is more sweetly insistent to us than all the voices which call us away from him.

◦━

The farewell command

John 13:33–5

> 'Little children, I am still going to be with you for a little while. You will search for me; and, as I said to the Jews, so now I say to you too: "You cannot go where I am going." I give you a new commandment, that you love one another; that you too love one another, as I have loved you; it is by this that all will know that you are my disciples – if you have love among each other.'

JESUS was laying down his farewell commandment to his disciples. The time was short; if they were ever to hear his voice, they must hear it now. He was going on a journey on which none might accompany him; he was taking a road that he had to walk alone; and before he went, he gave them the commandment that they must love one another as he had loved them. What does this mean for us, and for our relationships with one another? How did Jesus love his disciples?

(1) He loved his disciples *selflessly*. Even in the noblest human love, there remains some element of self. We so often think – maybe unconsciously – of what we are to get. We

think of the happiness we will receive, or of the loneliness we will suffer if love fails or is denied. So often we are thinking, what will this love do for me? So often at the back of things it is *our* happiness that we are seeking. But Jesus never thought of himself. His one desire was to give himself and all he had for those he loved.

(2) Jesus loved his disciples *sacrificially*. There was no limit to what his love would give or to where it would go. No demand that could be made upon it was too much. If love meant the cross, Jesus was prepared to go there. Sometimes we make the mistake of thinking that love is meant to give us happiness. So in the end it does, but love may well bring pain and demand a cross.

(3) Jesus loved his disciples *understandingly*. He knew his disciples through and through. We never really know people until we have lived with them. When we are meeting them only occasionally, we see them at their best. It is when we live with them that we find out their moods and their irritabilities and their weaknesses. Jesus had lived with his disciples day in and day out for many months and knew all that was to be known about them – and he still loved them. Sometimes we say that love is blind. That is not so, for the love that is blind can end in nothing but bleak and utter disillusionment. Real love is open-eyed. It loves, not what it imagines people to be, but what they are. The heart of Jesus is big enough to love us as we are.

(4) Jesus loved his disciples *forgivingly*. Their leader was to deny him. They were all to forsake him in his hour of need. They never really understood him. They were blind and insensitive, slow to learn, and lacking in understanding. In the end, they were miserable cowards. But Jesus held

nothing against them; there was no failure which he could not forgive. The love which has not learned to forgive cannot do anything else but shrivel and die. We are poor creatures, and there is a kind of fate in things which makes us hurt most of all those who love us best. For that very reason, all enduring love must be built on forgiveness, for without forgiveness it is bound to die.

❧

The traitor's bargain

Matthew 26:14–16

> Then one of the Twelve, called Judas Iscariot, went to the chief priests and said: 'What are you willing to give me, if I hand him over to you?' They settled with him for a sum of thirty shekels; and from that time he sought for an opportunity to betray him.

THE Jewish authorities wished to find a way in which to arrest Jesus without provoking riotous disturbances, and now that way was presented to them by the approach of Judas. There can be only three real reasons why Judas betrayed Jesus. All other suggestions are variations of these three.

(1) It may have been because of greed. According to Matthew and Mark, it was immediately after the anointing at Bethany that Judas struck his dreadful bargain; and when John tells his story of that event, he says that Judas made his protest against the anointing because he was a thief and pilfered from the money that was in the box (John 12:6).

If that is so, Judas struck one of the most dreadful bargains in history. The sum for which he agreed to betray Jesus was thirty *arguria*. An *argurion* was a *shekel*, and was the equivalent of about four days' wages. Judas, therefore, sold Jesus for a little under six months' pay. If greed was the cause of his act of treachery, it is the most terrible example in history of the depths which love of money can reach.

(2) It may have been because of bitter hatred, based on complete disillusionment. The Jews always had their dream of power; therefore they had their extreme nationalists who were prepared to go to any lengths of murder and violence to drive the Romans from Palestine. These nationalists were called the *sicarii*, the dagger-bearers, because they followed a deliberate policy of assassination. It may be that Judas was one such, and that he had looked on Jesus as the divinely sent leader who, with his miraculous powers, could lead the great rebellion. He may have seen that Jesus had deliberately taken another way, the way that led to a cross. And in his bitter disappointment, Judas' devotion may have turned first to disillusionment and then to a hatred which drove him to seek the death of the man from whom he had expected so much. Judas may have hated Jesus because he was not the Christ he wished him to be.

(3) It may be that Judas never intended Jesus to die. It may be that, as we have seen, he saw in Jesus the divine leader. He may have thought that Jesus was proceeding far too slowly; and he may have wished for nothing else than to force his hand. He may have betrayed Jesus with the intention of compelling him to act. That is in fact the view which best suits all the facts. And that would explain why Judas was shattered into suicide when his plan went wrong.

However we look at it, the tragedy of Judas is that he refused to accept Jesus as he was and tried to make him what he wanted him to be. It is not Jesus who can be changed by us, but we who must be changed by Jesus. We can never use him for our purposes; we must submit to be used for his. The tragedy of Judas is that of a man who thought he knew better than God.

~

The traitor's kiss

Luke 22:47–53

While Jesus was still speaking – look you – there came a crowd, and the man called Judas, one of the Twelve, was leading them. He came up to Jesus to kiss him; but Jesus said to him, 'Judas, is it with a kiss that you would betray the Son of Man?' When those who were around him saw what was going to happen, they said, 'Lord, shall we strike with the sword?' And one of them struck the servant of the high priest and cut off his ear. Jesus answered, 'Let it come even to this!' Jesus said to the chief priests and the Temple captains, and to the elders who had come to him, 'Have you come out with swords and cudgels as against a brigand? When I was daily with you in the Temple you did not lift your hand against me; but this is your hour, and the power of darkness is here.'

Judas had found a way to betray Jesus in such a way that the authorities could come upon him when the crowd was not there. He knew that Jesus was in the habit of going at nights to the garden on the hill, and there he led the emissaries of the Sanhedrin. The captain of the Temple, or the Sagan, as he was called, was the official who was responsible for the good order of the Temple; the captains of the Temple referred to here were his lieutenants who were responsible for carrying out the actual arrest of Jesus. When a disciple met a beloved Rabbi, he laid his right hand on the Rabbi's left shoulder and his left hand on the right shoulder and kissed him. It was the kiss of a disciple to a beloved master that Judas used as a sign of betrayal.

There were four different parties involved in this arrest, and their actions and reactions are very significant.

(1) There was Judas the traitor. He was the man who had *abandoned God* and entered into a league with Satan. It is only when people have put God out of their lives and taken Satan in, that they can sink to selling Christ.

(2) There were the Jews who had come to arrest Jesus. They were the men who were *blind to God*. When God incarnate came to this earth, all that they could think of was how to hustle him to a cross. They had so long chosen their own way and shut their ears to the voice of God and their eyes to his guidance that in the end they could not recognize him when he came. It is a terrible thing to be blind and deaf to God. As Elizabeth Barrett Browning wrote:

> *I too have strength –*
> *Strength to behold him and not worship him,*
> *Strength to fall from him and not to cry to him.*

God save us from a strength like that!

(3) There were the disciples. They were the men who *for the moment had forgotten God*. Their world had fallen in and they were sure the end had come. The last thing they

remembered at that moment was God; the only thing they thought of was the terrible situation into which they had come. Two things happen to those who forget God and leave him out of the situation. They become utterly terrified and completely disorganized. They lose the power to face life and to cope with it. In the time of trial, life is unlivable without God.

(4) There was Jesus. And Jesus was the one person in the whole scene who *remembered God*. The amazing thing about him in the last days was his absolute serenity once Gethsemane was over. In those days, even at his arrest, it was he who seemed to be in control; and even at his trial, it was he who was the judge. When we walk with God we can cope with any situation and look any foe in the eyes, unbowed and unafraid. It is only when we have bowed to God that we can talk and act like conquerors.

≈

The arrest in the garden

Matthew 26:50–6

> Then they came forward and laid hands on Jesus and held him. And, look you, one of these who was with Jesus stretched out his hand, and drew his sword, and struck the servant of the high priest, and cut off his ear. Then Jesus said to him: 'Put back your sword in its place; for all who take the sword shall perish by the sword. Or, do you not think that I am able to call on my Father, and he will on the spot send to my aid more than twelve regiments of angels? How then are the Scriptures to be

fulfilled that it must happen so?' At that hour Jesus said to the crowds: 'Have you come out with swords and cudgels to arrest me, as against a brigand? Daily I sat teaching in the Temple, and you did not lay hold on me. All this has happened that the writings of the prophets might be fulfilled.' Then all his disciples forsook him and fled.

JESUS would allow no resistance. Matthew simply tells us that one of the disciples drew a sword and, prepared to resist to the death and to sell his life dearly, wounded a servant of the high priest. When John tells the same story (John 18:10), he tells us that the disciple was Peter, and the servant was Malchus. The reason why John names Peter, and Matthew does not, may simply be that John was writing much later, and that when Matthew was writing it was still not safe to name the disciple who had sprung so quickly to his Master's defence. Here we have still another instance of the almost fantastic courage of Peter. He was willing to take on the mob alone; and let us always remember that it was after that, when he was a marked man, that Peter followed Jesus right into the courtyard of the high priest's house. But in all these incidents of the last hours it is on Jesus that our attention is fastened; and here we learn two things about him.

(1) His death was *by his own choice*. He need never have come to Jerusalem for the Passover Feast. Having come, he need never have followed his deliberate policy of magnificent defiance. Even in the garden, he could have slipped away and saved himself, for it was night, and there were many who would have smuggled him out of the city. Even here, he could have called down the might of God and destroyed his enemies. Every step of these last days makes it clearer and

clearer that Jesus laid down his life and that his life was not taken from him. Jesus died, not because his enemies killed him, but because he chose to die.

(2) He chose to die because he knew that his death was *the purpose of God*. He took this way because it was the very thing that had been foretold by the prophets. He took it because love is the only way. 'All who take the sword shall perish by the sword.' Violence can beget nothing but violence; one drawn sword can produce only another drawn sword to meet it. Jesus knew that war and might settle nothing, but produce only a train of evil, and beget a grim horde of children worse than themselves. He knew that God's purpose can be worked out only by sacrificial love. And history proved him right; for those who took him with violence, and who gloried in violence, and who would gladly have dipped their swords in Roman blood, saw forty years later their city destroyed forever, while the man who would not fight is enthroned forever in the hearts of men and women.

❧

A certain young man

Mark 14:51–2

> And a certain young man was following him, clothed in a
> linen sheet over his naked body. And they tried to seize him,
> but he left the linen sheet and escaped naked.

THESE are two strange and fascinating verses. At first sight they seem completely irrelevant. They seem to add nothing to the narrative and yet there must be some reason for their being there.

Matthew and Luke used Mark's Gospel as the basis of their work and they include in their gospels practically everything that is in Mark. But they do not include these two verses. That would seem to show that this incident was interesting to Mark and not really interesting to anyone else. Why then was this incident so interesting to Mark that he felt he must include it? The most probable answer is that the young man was Mark himself, and that this is his way of saying, 'I was there', without mentioning his own name at all.

When we read Acts we find that the meeting place and headquarters of the Jerusalem church was apparently in the house of Mary, the mother of John Mark (Acts 12:12). If that is so, it is at least probable that the upper room in which the Last Supper was eaten was in that same house. There could be no more natural place than that to be the centre of the Church. If we can assume that, there are two possibilities.

(1) It may be that Mark was actually present at the Last Supper. He was young, just a boy, and maybe no one really noticed him. But he was fascinated with Jesus, and when the company went out into the dark, he slipped out after them when he ought to have been in bed, with only the linen sheet over his naked body. It may be that all the time Mark was there in the shadows listening and watching. That would explain where the Gethsemane narrative came from. If the disciples were all asleep, how did anyone know about the struggle of soul that Jesus had there? It may be that the one witness was Mark as he stood silent in the shadows, watching with a boy's reverence the greatest hero he had ever known.

(2) From John's narrative, we know that Judas left the company before the meal was fully ended (John 13:30). It may be that it was to the upper room that Judas meant to lead the Temple police so that they might secretly arrest Jesus. But when Judas came back with the police, Jesus and his disciples were gone. Naturally there was recrimination and argument. The uproar wakened Mark. He heard Judas propose that they should try the garden of Gethsemane. Quickly Mark wrapped his bedsheet about him and sped through the night to the garden to warn Jesus. But he arrived too late, and in the scuffle that followed was very nearly arrested himself.

Whatever may be true, we may take it as fairly certain that Mark put in these two verses because they were about himself. He could never forget that night. He was too humble to put his own name in, but in this way he wrote his signature and said, to anyone who could read between the lines, 'I, too, when I was a boy, was there.'

Jesus before Annas

John 18:12–14, 19–24

The company of soldiers and their commander and the officers of the Jews took Jesus, and bound him, and led him first of all to Annas. He was the father-in-law of Caiaphas who was high priest in that year. It was Caiaphas who had advised the Jews that it was better that one man should die for the people … The high priest questioned Jesus about his disciples and about his teaching. Jesus answered him: 'I spoke openly in the world.

> *I taught at all times in the synagogue and in the precincts of the*
> *Temple, where all the Jews assemble, and I spoke nothing in*
> *secret. Why do you ask me questions? Ask those who heard me*
> *what I said to them. See! These know what I have said.' When*
> *he had said these things, one of the officers who was standing*
> *by dealt Jesus a blow. 'Do you answer the high priest like this?'*
> *he said. Jesus answered: 'If I have spoken ill, produce evidence*
> *about the ill; if I have spoken well, why do you strike me?' So*
> *Annas sent him bound to Caiaphas, the high priest.*

For the sake of keeping the narrative continuous, we take together the two passages in John's Gospel which deal with the trial before Annas.

Only John tells us that Jesus was brought first of all to Annas. Annas was a notorious character. The nineteenth-century scholar Alfred Edersheim writes of him: 'No figure is better known in contemporary Jewish history than that of Annas; no person deemed more fortunate or successful, but none also more generally execrated than the late high priest.' Annas was the power behind the throne in Jerusalem. He himself had been high priest from AD 6 to 15. Four of his sons had also held the high priesthood, and Caiaphas was his son-in-law. That very fact is itself suggestive and illuminating. There had been a time, when the Jews were free, when the high priest had held office for life; but when the Roman governors came, the office became matter for contention, intrigue, bribery and corruption. It now went to the greatest sycophant and the highest bidder, to the man who was most willing to toe the line with the Roman governor. The high priest was the arch-collaborator, the man who bought comfort, ease, prestige and power not only with bribes but also with close co-operation with his country's masters. The family of Annas was immensely rich, and one by one they had intrigued and bribed their way into office, while Annas remained the power behind it all.

Even the way in which Annas made his money was most probably disgraceful. In the Court of the Gentiles, there were the sellers of victims for the sacrifices, those sellers whom Jesus had driven out. They were not traders; they were extortioners. Every victim offered in the Temple had to be without spot and blemish. There were inspectors to see that it was so. If a victim was bought outside the Temple, it was certain that a flaw would be found. The worshipper was then directed to buy at the Temple booths where the victims had already been examined and where there was no risk of rejection. That would have been convenient and helpful but for one thing. Inside the Temple, a pair of doves could cost as much as fifteen times what could have been paid if bought outside. The whole business was sheer exploitation; and the shops where the Temple victims were sold were called the Bazaars of Annas. They were the property of the family of Annas; it was by the exploitation of the worshippers, by trading on the sacred sacrifices, that Annas had amassed a fortune. The Jews themselves hated the household of Annas. There is a passage in the *Talmud* which says: 'Woe to the house of Annas! Woe to their serpent's hiss! They are high priests; their sons are keepers of the treasury; their sons-in-law are guardians of the Temple; and their servants beat the people with staves.' Annas and his household were notorious.

Now we can see why Annas arranged that Jesus should be brought first to him. Jesus was the man who had attacked Annas' vested interest; he had cleared the Temple of the sellers of victims and had hit Annas where it hurt – in his pocket. Annas wanted to be the first to gloat over the capture of this disturbing Galilaean.

The examination before Annas was a mockery of justice. It was an essential regulation of the Jewish law that a prisoner must be asked no question which would incriminate him. Maimonides, the great Jewish medieval scholar, lays it down: 'Our true law does not inflict the penalty of death upon a sinner by his own confession.' Annas violated the principles of Jewish justice when he questioned Jesus. It was precisely of this that Jesus reminded him. Jesus said: 'Don't ask me questions. Ask those who heard me.' He was, in effect, saying: 'Take your evidence about me in the proper and legal way. Examine your witnesses, which you have every right to do; stop examining me, which you have no right to do.' When Jesus said that, one of the officers hit him a slap across the face. He said, in effect, 'Are you trying to teach the high priest how to conduct a trial?' Jesus' answer was: 'If I have said or taught anything illegal, witnesses should be called. I have only stated the law. Why hit me for that?'

Jesus never had any hope of justice. The self-interest of Annas and his colleagues had been touched; and Jesus was condemned before he was tried. When people are engaged on evil ways, their only desire is to eliminate anyone who opposes them. If they cannot do it by fair means, they are compelled to resort to foul.

The man who sentenced Jesus to death

Matthew 27:1–2, 11–26

When the morning came, all the chief priests and elders of the people took counsel against Jesus, to put him to death; so they bound him, and led him away, and handed him over to Pilate the governor …

Jesus stood before the governor, and the governor put the question to him: 'Are you the King of the Jews?' Jesus said to him: 'You say so.' While he was being accused by the chief priests and the elders, he returned no answer. Then Pilate said to him: 'Do you not hear the evidence which they are stating against you?' Jesus answered not a single word, so that the governor was much amazed. At the time of the Feast the governor was in the habit of releasing one prisoner to the crowd, a prisoner whom they wished. At that time he was holding a very well-known prisoner called Barabbas. So, when they were assembled, Pilate said to them: 'Whom do you wish me to release to you? Barabbas? Or, Jesus who is called Christ?' For he was well aware that they had delivered Jesus to him because of malice. While he was sitting on his judgment seat, his wife sent a message to him. 'Have nothing to do with this just man,' she said, 'for today I have had an extraordinary experience in a dream because of him.' The chief priests and the elders persuaded the crowds to ask for the release of Barabbas, and the destruction of Jesus. 'Which of the two', said the governor, 'am I to release to you?' 'Barabbas,' they said. 'What then,' said Pilate to them, 'am I to do with Jesus who is called Christ?' 'Let him be crucified,' they all said. 'What evil has he done?' he said. They kept shouting all the more: 'Let him be crucified.' When

*Pilate saw that it was hopeless to do anything, and that rather
a disturbance was liable to arise, he took water, and washed
his hands in presence of the crowd. 'I am innocent of the blood
of this just man,' he said. 'You must see to it.' All the people
answered: 'Let the responsibility for his blood be on us and on
our children.' Then he released Barabbas to them; but he had
Jesus scourged, and handed him over to be crucified.*

THE first two verses of this passage describe what must have
been a very brief meeting of the Sanhedrin, held early in the
morning, with a view to formulating finally an official charge
against Jesus. The necessity for this lay in the fact that, while
the Jews could themselves deal with an ordinary charge,
they could not inflict the death penalty. That was a sentence
which could be pronounced only by the Roman governor,
and carried out by the Roman authorities. The Sanhedrin had
therefore to formulate a charge with which they could go to
Pilate and demand the death of Jesus.

Matthew does not tell us what that charge was; but Luke
does. In the Sanhedrin, the charge which was levelled against
Jesus was a charge of blasphemy (Matthew 26:65–6). But no
one knew better than the Jewish authorities that that was
a charge to which Pilate would not listen. He would tell
them to go away and settle their own religious quarrels. So,
as Luke tells us, they appeared before Pilate with a threefold
charge, every item in which was a lie, and a deliberate lie.
They charged Jesus first with being a revolutionary, second,
with inciting the people not to pay their taxes, and third,
with claiming to be a king (Luke 23:2). They fabricated three
political charges, all of them conscious lies, because they knew
that only on such charges would Pilate act.

So, everything hung on the attitude of Pilate. What kind of man was this Roman governor?

Pilate was officially *procurator* of the province; and he was directly responsible not to the Roman senate but to the Roman emperor. He must have been at least twenty-seven years of age, for that was the minimum age for taking up the office of procurator. He must have been a man of considerable experience, for there was a ladder of offices, including military command, up which a man must climb until he qualified to become a governor. Pilate must have been a tried and tested soldier and administrator. He became procurator of Judaea in AD 26 and held office for ten years, when he was recalled from his post.

When Pilate came to Judaea, he found trouble in plenty, and much of it was of his own making. His great handicap was that he was completely out of sympathy with the Jews. More, he was contemptuous of what he would have called their irrational and fanatical prejudices, and what they would have called their principles. The Romans knew the intensity of Jewish religion and the unbreakable character of Jewish belief, and very wisely had always dealt with the Jews with kid gloves. Pilate arrogantly proposed to take a hard line.

He began with trouble. The Roman headquarters were in Caesarea. The Roman standards were not flags; they were poles with the Roman eagle, or the image of the reigning emperor, on top. In deference to the Jewish hatred of graven images, every previous governor had removed the eagles and the images from the standards before he marched into Jerusalem on his state visits. Pilate refused to do so. The result was such bitter opposition and such intransigence that Pilate in the end was forced to yield, for it is not possible either to arrest or to slaughter a whole nation.

Later, Pilate decided that Jerusalem needed a better water supply – a wise decision. To that end, he constructed a new aqueduct – but he took money from the Temple treasury to pay for it.

Philo, the great Jewish Alexandrian scholar, has a character study of Pilate – and Philo, remember, was not a Christian, but was speaking from the Jewish point of view. The Jews, Philo tells us, had threatened to exercise their right to report Pilate to the emperor for his misdeeds. This threat 'exasperated Pilate to the greatest possible degree, as he feared lest they might go on an embassy to the emperor, and might impeach him with respect to other particulars of his government – his corruption, his acts of insolence, his rapine, his habit of insulting people, his cruelty, his continual murders of people untried and uncondemned, and his never-ending gratuitous and most grievous inhumanity.' Pilate had a bad record in dealing with the Jews, who held him in complete contempt; and the fact that they could report him made his position entirely insecure.

We follow the career of Pilate to the end. In the end, he was recalled to Rome on account of his savagery in an incident in Samaria. A certain impostor had summoned the people to Mount Gerizim with the claim that he would show them the sacred vessels which Moses had hidden there. Unfortunately many of the crowd came armed, and assembled in a village called Tirabatha. Pilate fell on them and slaughtered them with quite unnecessary savagery, for it was a harmless enough movement. The Samaritans lodged a complaint with Vitellius, the legate of Syria, who was Pilate's immediate superior, and Vitellius ordered him to return to Rome to answer for his conduct.

When Pilate was on his way to Rome, Tiberius the emperor died; and it appears that Pilate never came to trial. Legend has it that in the end he committed suicide; his body was flung into the Tiber, but the evil spirits so troubled the river that the Romans took the body to Gaul and threw it into the Rhône. Pilate's so-called tomb is still shown in the French town of Vienne. The same thing happened there; and the body was finally taken to a place near Lausanne and buried in a pit in the mountains. Opposite Lucerne there is a hill called Mount Pilatus. Originally the mountain was called *Pileatus*, which means *wearing a cap of clouds*, but because it was connected with Pilate the name was changed to *Pilatus*.

Later Christian legend was sympathetic to Pilate and tended to place all the blame for the death of Jesus on the Jews. Not unnaturally, legend came to hold that Pilate's wife, who it is said was a Jewish convert, and was called Claudia Procula, became a Christian. It was even held that Pilate himself became a Christian; and to this day the Coptic Church ranks both Pilate and his wife as saints.

We conclude this study of Pilate with a very interesting document. Pilate must have sent a report of the trial and death of Jesus to Rome; that would happen in the normal course of administration. An apocryphal book called The Acts of Peter and Paul contains an alleged copy of that report. This report is actually referred to by the early Christian writers Tertullian, Justin Martyr and Eusebius. The report as we have it can hardly be genuine, but it is interesting to read it:

Pontius Pilate unto Claudius greeting

There befell of late a matter of which I myself made trial; for the Jews through envy have punished themselves and their posterity with fearful judgments of their own fault; for whereas their fathers had promises that their God would send them out of heaven his Holy One, who should of right be called king, and did promise he would send him on earth by a virgin; he then came when I was governor of Judaea, and they beheld him enlightening the blind, cleansing lepers, healing the palsied, driving devils out of men, raising the dead, rebuking the winds, walking on the waves of the sea dry-shod, and doing many other wonders, and all the people of the Jews calling him the Son of God; the chief priests therefore moved with envy against him, took him and delivered him unto me and brought against him one false accusation after another, saying that he was a sorcerer and that he did things contrary to the law.

But I, believing that these things were so, having scourged him, delivered him to their will; and they crucified him, and, when he was buried, they set their guards upon him. But while my soldiers watched him, he rose again on the third day; yet so much was the malice of the Jews kindled, that they gave money to the soldiers saying: Say ye that his disciples stole away his body. But they, though they took the money, were not able to keep silence concerning that which had come to pass, for they also have testified that they saw him arisen, and that they received money from the Jews. And these things have I reported unto thy mightiness for this cause, lest some

other should lie unto thee, and thou shouldest deem right
to believe the false tales of the Jews.

Although that report is no doubt mere legend, Pilate certainly
knew that Jesus was innocent; but his past misdeeds gave the
Jews a lever with which to compel him to do their will against
his wishes and his sense of justice.

Pilate's losing struggle

Matthew 27:1–2, 11–26 (*contd*)

THIS whole passage gives the impression of a man fighting a
losing battle. It is clear that Pilate did not wish to condemn
Jesus. Certain things emerge.

(1) Pilate was clearly impressed by Jesus. Plainly he did
not take seriously the claim to be the King of the Jews. He
knew a revolutionary when he saw one, and Jesus was no
revolutionary. His dignified silence made Pilate feel that it
was not Jesus but he himself who was on trial. Pilate was a
man who felt the power of Jesus – and was afraid to submit
to it. There are still those who are afraid to be as Christian as
they know they ought to be.

(2) Pilate sought some way of escape. It appears to have
been the custom at the time of the Feast for a prisoner to be
released. In jail there was a certain Barabbas. He was not a
minor criminal; he was most probably either a brigand or a
political revolutionary.

There are two interesting speculations about him. His
name *Barabbas* means *Son of the Father*; *father* was a title by
which the greatest Rabbis were known; it may well be that

Barabbas was the son of an ancient and distinguished family who had kicked over the traces and embarked on a career of magnificent crime. Such a man would make crime glamorous and would appeal to the people.

Still more interesting is the near-certainty that Barabbas was also called Jesus. Some of the very oldest versions of the New Testament, for example the ancient Syriac and Armenian versions, call him *Jesus Barabbas*; and those two early interpreters of Scripture, Origen and Jerome, both knew of that reading, and felt it might be correct. It is a curious thing that twice Pilate refers to *Jesus who is called Christ* (verses 17 and 22), as if to distinguish him from some other Jesus. Jesus was a common name; it is the same name as Joshua. And the dramatic shout of the crowd most likely was: 'Not Jesus Christ, but Jesus Barabbas.'

Pilate sought an escape, but the crowd chose the violent criminal and rejected the gentle Christ. They preferred the man of violence to the man of love.

(3) Pilate sought to escape the responsibility for condemning Jesus. There is that strange and tragic picture of him washing his hands. That was a Jewish custom. There is a strange regulation in Deuteronomy 21:1–9. If a dead body was found, and it was not known who the killer was, measurements were to be taken to find what was the nearest town or village. The elders of that town or village had to sacrifice a heifer and to wash their hands to rid them of the guilt.

Pilate was warned by his sense of justice, he was warned by his conscience, he was warned by the dream of his troubled wife; but Pilate could not stand against the mob; and Pilate made the futile gesture of washing his hands. Legend has it that to this day there are times when Pilate's ghost emerges from its tomb and goes through the action of the handwashing once again.

There is one thing of which we can never rid ourselves – and that is responsibility. It is never possible for Pilate or anyone else to say: 'I wash my hands of all responsibility', for that is something that no one and nothing can take away.

This picture of Pilate provokes in our minds pity rather than loathing; for here was a man so enmeshed in his past, and rendered helpless to such an extent by it, that he was unable to take the stand he ought to have taken. Pilate is a figure of tragedy rather than of villainy.

The soldiers' mockery

Mark 15:16–20

> *The soldiers led Jesus away into the hall, which is the Praetorium, and they called together the whole company. They clad him in a purple robe, and they plaited a crown of thorns and put it on him, and they began to salute him, 'Hail! King of the Jews!' And they struck his head with a reed, and they spat on him, and they knelt down before him and worshipped him. And after they had made sport of him, they took off the purple robe, and clad him in his own clothes. And they led him away to crucify him.*

THE Roman ritual of condemnation was fixed. The judge said *Illum duci ad crucem placet*, 'The sentence is that this man should be taken to a cross.' Then he turned to the guard and said, *I, miles, expedi crucem,* 'Go, soldier, and prepare the cross.' It was when the cross was being prepared that Jesus was in the hands of the soldiers. The Praetorium was the residence of the governor, his headquarters, and the soldiers involved would be the headquarters' cohort of the guard. We would do well to remember that Jesus had already undergone the agony of scourging before this horseplay of the soldiers began.

It may well be that of all that happened to him this hurt Jesus least. The actions of the Jews had been venomous with hatred. The consent of Pilate had been a cowardly evasion of responsibility. There was cruelty in the action of the soldiers but no malice. To them Jesus was only another man for a cross, and they carried out their barrack-room pantomime of royalty and worship, not with any malice, but as a coarse jest.

It was the beginning of much mockery to come. Always the Christian was liable to be regarded as a jest. Scribbled on the walls of Pompeii, whose walls are still chalked with coarse jests today, there is a picture of a Christian kneeling before a donkey and below it scrawled the words, 'Anaximenes worships his God.' If people ever make a jest of our Christianity, it will help to remember that they did it to Jesus in a way that is worse than anything likely to happen to us.

The cross

Mark 15:21–8

And they impressed into service a man called Simon of Cyrene, who was passing by, on his way in from the country, the father of Alexander and Rufus, and they made him carry his cross. So they brought him to the place Golgotha, which means the place of a skull. They offered him wine mingled with myrrh, but he would not take it. They crucified him. And they divided out his garments, throwing dice for them to decide who should take what. It was 9 am when they crucified him. And the inscription of the charge against him was written on the cross – 'The King of the Jews'. With him they crucified two brigands, one on his right hand and one on his left.

THE routine of crucifixion did not alter. When the cross was prepared the criminal had himself to carry it to the place of execution. He was placed in the middle of a hollow square of four soldiers. In front marched a soldier carrying a board stating the crime of which the prisoner was guilty. The board was afterwards affixed to the cross. They took not the shortest but the longest way to the place of execution. They followed every possible street and lane so that as many as possible should see and take warning. When they reached the place of crucifixion, the cross was laid flat on the ground. The prisoner was stretched upon it and nailed to it. The nails were usually driven through the wrists. The feet were not nailed but only loosely bound. Between the prisoner's legs projected a ledge of wood called the saddle, to take his weight when the cross was raised upright – otherwise the nails would have torn through the wrists. The cross was then lifted upright and set in its socket – and the criminal was left to die. The cross was not tall. It was shaped like the letter T, and had no top piece at all. Sometimes prisoners hung for as long as a week, slowly dying of hunger and of thirst, suffering sometimes to the point of actual madness.

This must have been a grim day for Simon of Cyrene. Palestine was an occupied country and any man might be pressed into the Roman service for any task. The sign of this was a tap on the shoulder with the flat of a Roman spear. Simon was from Cyrene in Africa. No doubt he had come from that far-off land for the Passover. No doubt he had scraped and saved for many years in order to come. No doubt he was gratifying the ambition of a lifetime to eat one Passover in Jerusalem. Then this happened to him.

At the moment Simon must have bitterly resented it. He must have hated the Romans, and hated this criminal whose cross he was being forced to carry. But we may legitimately speculate what happened to Simon. It may be that it was his intention when he got to Golgotha to fling the cross down on the ground and hasten as quickly as he could from the scene. But perhaps it did not turn out that way. Perhaps he lingered on because something about Jesus fascinated him.

He is described as *the father of Alexander and Rufus*. The people for whom the gospel was written must have been meant to recognize him by this description. It is most likely that Mark's gospel was first written for the church at Rome. Now let us turn to Paul's letter to Rome and read Romans 16:13. 'Greet Rufus, chosen in the Lord; and greet his mother – a mother to me also.' Rufus was so eminent a Christian that he was *chosen in the Lord*. The mother of Rufus was so dear to Paul that he could call her his own mother. Things must have happened to Simon on Golgotha.

Now turn to Acts 13:1. There is a list of the men of Antioch who sent Paul and Barnabas out on that epoch-making first mission to the Gentiles. The name of one is *Simeon who was called Niger. Simeon* is another form of *Simon. Niger* was the regular name for a man of dark skin who came from Africa, and Cyrene is in Africa. Here it may well be that we are meeting Simon again. Maybe Simon's experience on the way to Golgotha bound his heart forever to Jesus. Maybe it made him a Christian. Maybe in the after days he was a leader in Antioch and instrumental in the first mission to the Gentiles. Maybe it was because Simon was compelled to carry the cross of Jesus that the first mission to the Gentiles took place. That would mean that *we* are Christians because one day a Passover pilgrim from Cyrene, to his bitter resentment at the time, was pressed by a nameless Roman officer to carry his cross for Jesus.

They offered Jesus drugged wine and he would not drink it. A company of pious and merciful women in Jerusalem came to every crucifixion and gave the criminals a drink of drugged wine to ease the terrible pain. They offered this to Jesus – and he refused it. When Dr Johnson was ill with his last illness, he asked his doctor to tell him honestly if he could recover. The doctor said he could not without a miracle. 'Then', said Johnson, 'I will take no more physic, not even opiates, for I have prayed that I may render up my soul to God unclouded.' Jesus was resolved to taste death at its bitterest and to go to God with open eyes.

The soldiers threw dice for his clothes. We have seen how the prisoner was marched to the place of crucifixion amid the four soldiers. These soldiers had as their 'perk' the clothes of the criminal. Now, a Jew wore *five* articles of clothing – the inner robe, the outer robe, the sandals, the girdle and the turban. When the four lesser things had been assigned, that left the great outer robe. It would have been useless to cut it up, so the soldiers gambled for it in the shadow of the cross.

Jesus was crucified between two thieves. It was a symbol of his whole life that even at the end he kept company with sinners.

～

There they crucified him

Luke 23:32–8

Two others who were criminals were brought to be put to death with Jesus. When they came to the place which is called the place of a skull, there they crucified him, and the two criminals, one on his right hand, and one on his left. And Jesus said, 'Father, forgive them, for they do not know what they are doing.' And, as they divided his garments, they cast lots for them. The people stood watching, and the rulers gibed at him. 'He saved others,' they said. 'Let him save himself if he really is the Anointed One of God, the chosen one.' The soldiers also mocked him, coming and offering vinegar to him, and saying, 'If you are the King of the Jews save yourself.' There was also an inscription over him, 'This is the King of the Jews'.

THE inscription set upon the cross was the same placard as was carried before a man as he marched through the streets to the place of crucifixion.

Jesus said many wonderful things, but rarely anything more wonderful than, 'Father, forgive them, for they know not what they do.' Christian forgiveness is an amazing thing. When Stephen was being stoned to death he too prayed, 'Lord, do not hold this sin against them' (Acts 7:60). There is nothing so lovely and nothing so rare as Christian forgiveness. When the unforgiving spirit is threatening to turn our hearts to bitterness, let us hear again our Lord asking forgiveness for those who crucified him and his servant Paul saying to his friends, 'Be kind to one another, tenderhearted, forgiving one another, as God in Christ has forgiven you' (Ephesians 4:32).

The idea that this terrible thing was done in ignorance runs through the New Testament. Peter later said to the people, 'I know that you acted in ignorance' (Acts 3:17). Paul said that they crucified Jesus because they did not know him (Acts 13:27). Marcus Aurelius, the great Roman emperor and Stoic saint, used to say to himself every morning, 'Today you will meet all kinds of unpleasant people; they will hurt you, and injure you, and insult you; but you cannot live like that; you know better, for you are a man in whom the spirit of God dwells.' Others may have in their hearts the unforgiving spirit, others may sin in ignorance; but we know better. We are Christ's men and women; and we must forgive as he forgave.

The promise of Paradise

Luke 23:39–43

One of the criminals who were hanged kept hurling insults at Jesus. 'Are you not the Anointed One?' he said. 'Save yourself and us.' The other rebuked him. 'Do you not even fear God?' he said. 'For we too are under the same sentence and justly so, for we have done things which deserve the reward that we are reaping; but this man has done nothing unseemly.' And he

said, 'Jesus, remember me when you come into your kingdom.'
He said to him, 'This is the truth – I tell you – today you will
be with me in Paradise.'

IT was of set and deliberate purpose that the authorities
crucified Jesus between two known criminals. It was
deliberately so staged to humiliate Jesus in front of the crowd
and to rank him with robbers.

Legend has been busy with the penitent thief. He is called
variously Dismas, Demas and Dumachus. One legend makes
him a Judaean Robin Hood who robbed the rich to give to
the poor. The loveliest legend tells how the holy family were
attacked by robbers when they fled with the child Jesus
from Bethlehem to Egypt. Jesus was saved by the son of the
captain of the robber band. The baby was so lovely that the
young brigand could not bear to lay hands on him but set
him free, saying, 'O most blessed of children, if ever there
come a time for having mercy on me, then remember me
and forget not this hour.' That robber youth who had saved
Jesus as a baby met him again on Calvary; and this time
Jesus saved him.

The word Paradise is a Persian word meaning *a walled
garden*. When a Persian king wished to do one of his subjects
a very special honour he made him a companion of the garden
which meant he was chosen to walk in the garden with the
king. It was more than immortality that Jesus promised the
penitent thief. He promised him the honoured place of a
companion of the garden in the courts of heaven.

Surely this story tells us above all that it is never too late
to turn to Christ. There are other things of which we must
say, 'The time for that is past. I am grown too old now.' But we

can never say that of turning to Jesus Christ. So long as our
hearts continue to beat, the invitation of Christ still stands. It
is literally true that while there is life there is hope.

***

The triumphant ending

John 19:28–30

> *After that, when Jesus knew that everything was completed,
> he said, in order that the Scripture might be fulfilled: 'I thirst.'
> There was a vessel standing there full of vinegar. So they put
> a sponge soaked in vinegar on a hyssop reed, and put it to
> his mouth. When he had received the vinegar, Jesus said: 'It
> is finished.' And he leaned his head back, and gave up his
> spirit.*

In this passage, John brings us face to face with two things
about Jesus.

(1) He brings us face to face with his human suffering;
when Jesus was on the cross, he knew the agony of thirst.
When John was writing his gospel, round about AD 100, a
certain tendency had arisen in religious and philosophical
thought, called Gnosticism. One of its great tenets was that
spirit was altogether good and matter altogether evil. Certain
conclusions followed. One was that God, who was pure
spirit, could never take upon himself a body, because that
was matter, and matter was evil. They therefore taught that
Jesus never had a real body. They said that he was only a
phantom. They said, for instance, that when Jesus walked, his

feet left no prints on the ground, because he was pure spirit in a phantom body.

They went on to argue that God could never really suffer, and that therefore Jesus never really suffered but went through the whole experience of the cross without any real pain. When the Gnostics thought like that, they believed they were honouring God and honouring Jesus; but they were really destroying Jesus. If he was ever to redeem humanity, he must become human. He had to become what we are in order to make us what he is. That is why John stresses the fact that Jesus felt thirst; he wished to show that he was really human and really underwent the agony of the cross. John goes out of his way to stress the real humanity and the real suffering of Jesus.

(2) But, equally, he brings us face to face with the triumph of Jesus. When we compare the four gospels, we find a most illuminating thing. The other three do not tell us that Jesus said: 'It is finished.' But they do tell us that he died with a great shout upon his lips (Matthew 27:50; Mark 15:37; Luke 23:46). On the other hand, John does not speak of the great cry, but does say that Jesus' last words were: 'It is finished.' The explanation is that the great shout and the words 'It is finished' are one and the same thing. 'It is finished' is one word in Greek – *tetelestai* – and Jesus died with a shout of triumph on his lips. He did not say 'It is finished' in weary defeat; he said it as one who shouts for joy because the victory is won. He seemed to be broken on the cross, but he knew that his victory was won.

The last sentence of this passage makes the point even clearer. John says that Jesus leaned back his head and gave up his spirit. John uses the word which might be used for settling back upon a pillow. For Jesus, the strife was over and the battle was won; and even on the cross, he knew the joy of victory and the rest of the man who has completed his task and can lean back, content and at peace.

Two further things we must notice in this passage. John traces back Jesus' cry, 'I thirst,' to the fulfilment of a verse in the Old Testament. He is thinking of Psalm 69:21. 'They gave me poison for food, and for my thirst they gave me vinegar to drink.'

The second thing is another of John's hidden things. He tells us that it was on a hyssop reed that they put the sponge containing the vinegar. Now a hyssop reed is an unlikely thing to use for such a purpose, for it was only a stalk, like strong grass, and at the most two feet long. So unlikely is it that some scholars have thought that it is a mistake for a very similar word which means a *lance* or a *spear*. But it was *hyssop* which John wrote and *hyssop* which John meant. When we go centuries back to the first Passover when the children of Israel left their slavery in Egypt, we remember how the angel of death was to walk abroad that night and to slay every first-born son of the Egyptians. We remember how the Israelites were to slay the Passover lamb and were to smear the doorposts of their houses with its blood so that the avenging angel of death would *pass over* their houses. And the ancient instruction was: '*Take a bunch of hyssop*, dip it in the blood that is in the basin, and touch the lintel and the two doorposts with the blood in the basin' (Exodus 12:22). It was the blood of the Passover lamb which saved the people of God; it was the blood of Jesus which was to save the world from sin. The very mention of *hyssop* would take the thoughts of any Jew back to the saving blood of the Passover lamb; and this was John's way of saying that Jesus was the great Passover Lamb of God whose death was to save the whole world from sin.

The blazing revelation

Matthew 27:51–6

> And, look you, the veil of the Temple was rent in two from top to bottom, and the earth was shaken, and the rocks were split, and the tombs were opened, and the bodies of many of God's dedicated ones were raised, and they came out of the tombs after his resurrection and came into the holy city and appeared to many. The centurion and those who were watching Jesus with him saw the earthquake and the things that had happened, and they were exceedingly afraid. 'Truly,' they said, 'this man was the Son of God.'
>
> Many women were there watching from a distance. They were the women who had followed Jesus from Galilee, giving their service to him. Among them were Mary from Magdala, and Mary the mother of James and Joses [Joseph], and the mother of the sons of Zebedee.

This passage falls into three sections.

(1) There is the story of the amazing things that happened as Jesus died. Whether or not we are meant to take these things literally, they teach us two great truths.

(a) The Temple veil was rent from top to bottom. That was the veil which covered the Holy of Holies; that was the veil beyond which no one could penetrate, except the high priest on the Day of Atonement; that was the veil behind which the Spirit of God dwelt. There is symbolism here. Up to this time, God had been hidden and remote, and no one knew what he was like. But in the death of Jesus we see the hidden love of God, and the way to the presence of God once barred to everyone is now opened to all. The life and the death of Jesus show us what God is like and remove forever the veil which concealed him from men and women.

(b) The tombs were opened. The symbolism of this is that Jesus conquered death. In dying and in rising again, he destroyed the power of the grave. Because of his life, his death and his resurrection, the tomb has lost its power, and the grave has lost its terror, and death has lost its tragedy. For we are certain that because he lives we shall live also.

(2) There is the story of the adoration of the centurion. There is only one thing to be said about this. Jesus had said: 'I, when I am lifted up from the earth, will draw all people to myself' (John 12:32). He foretold the magnetic power of the cross; and the centurion was its first fruit. The cross had moved him to see the majesty of Jesus as nothing else had been able to do.

(3) There is the simple statement concerning the women who saw the end. All the disciples forsook him and fled, but the women remained. It has been said that, unlike the men, the women had nothing to fear, for so low was the public position of women that no one would take any notice of women disciples. There is more to it than that. They were there because they loved Jesus – and for them, as for so many, perfect love had cast out all fear.

⚬⚮

The last gifts to Jesus

John 19:38–42

> After that, Joseph from Arimathaea, who because of fear
> of the Jews was a secret disciple of Jesus, asked Pilate to
> be allowed to take away Jesus' body, and Pilate gave him
> permission to do so. So he came and took his body away.
> Nicodemus, who first came to Jesus by night, came too,
> bringing a mixture of myrrh and aloes, about 100 pounds in
> weight. So they took Jesus' body and they wrapped it in linen
> clothes with spices, as it is the Jewish custom to lay a body
> in the tomb. There was a garden in the place where he was
> crucified; and in the garden there was a new tomb in which
> no one had ever been laid. So they laid Jesus there, because
> it was the day of preparation for the Sabbath, because the
> tomb was near at hand.

So Jesus died, and what had to be done now must be done
quickly, for the Sabbath was almost begun and on the Sabbath
no work could be done. The friends of Jesus were poor and
could not have given him a fitting burial; but two people
came forward.

Joseph of Arimathaea was one. He had always been a
disciple of Jesus; he was a great man and a member of the
Sanhedrin, and up to now he had kept his discipleship
secret for he was afraid to make it known. Nicodemus was
the other. It was the Jewish custom to wrap the bodies of
the dead in linen clothes and to put sweet spices between
the folds of the linen. Nicodemus brought enough spices
for the burial of a king. So Joseph gave to Jesus a tomb;

and Nicodemus gave him the clothes to wear within the tomb.

There is both tragedy and glory here.

(1) There is tragedy. Both Nicodemus and Joseph were members of the Sanhedrin, but they were secret disciples of Jesus. Either they had absented themselves from the meeting of the Sanhedrin which examined him and formulated the charge against him, or they had sat silent through it all. What a difference it would have made to Jesus, if, among these condemning, hectoring voices, one voice had been raised in his support. What a difference it would have made to see loyalty on one face amid that sea of bleak, venomous and hostile faces. But Nicodemus and Joseph were afraid.

We so often leave our tributes until people are dead. How much greater would loyalty in life have been than a new tomb and a shroud fit for a king. One flower in life is worth all the wreaths in the world in death; one word of love and praise and thanks in life is worth all the tributes in the world when life is gone.

(2) But there is glory here, too. The death of Jesus had done for Joseph and Nicodemus what not even his life could do. No sooner had Jesus died on the cross than Joseph forgot his fear and confronted the Roman governor with a request for the body. No sooner had Jesus died on the cross than Nicodemus was there to bring a tribute that everyone could see. The cowardice, the hesitation, the prudent concealment were gone.

Those who had been afraid when Jesus was alive declared for him in a way that all could see as soon as he was dead. Jesus had not been dead an hour when his own prophecy came true: 'And I, when I am lifted up from the earth, will draw all people to myself' (John 12:32). It may be that the silence of Nicodemus or his absence from the Sanhedrin brought sorrow to Jesus; but it is certain that he knew of the way in which they cast their fear aside after the cross, and it is certain that already his heart was glad, for already the power of the cross had begun to operate, and already it was drawing all people to him. The power of the cross was even then turning the coward into the hero, and the waverer into the man who took an irrevocable decision for Christ.

The great discovery

Matthew 28:1–10

> Late on the Sabbath, when the first day of the week was beginning to dawn, Mary from Magdala and the other Mary came to see the tomb. And, look you, there was a great earthquake; for the angel of the Lord descended from heaven and came and rolled away the stone, and sat upon it. His appearance was like lightning, and his garment was as white as snow. Those who were watching were shaken with fear, and became as dead men. The angel said to the women: 'Do not be afraid; for I know that you are looking for Jesus who was crucified. He is not here; for he is risen, as he said he would. Come, see the place where the Lord lay. Go quickly and tell his disciples: "He is risen from among the

dead. And, look you, he goes before you into Galilee; there you will see him." Look you, I have told you.' So they quickly went away from the tomb with fear and with great joy, and they ran to tell the news to his disciples. And, look you, Jesus met them. 'Greetings!' he said. And they came and held him by the feet, and worshipped him. Then Jesus said to them: 'Fear not! Go, tell my brothers to go away into Galilee, and there they will see me.'

HERE we have Matthew's story of the empty tomb. And there is something peculiarly fitting in that Mary Magdalene and the other Mary should be the first to receive the news of the risen Lord and to encounter him. They had been there at the cross; they had been there when he was laid in the tomb; and now they were receiving love's reward; they were the first to know the joy of the resurrection.

As we read this story of the first two people in the world to be confronted with the fact of the empty tomb and the risen Christ, three imperatives seem to spring out of it.

(1) They are urged to *believe*. The thing is so staggering that it might seem beyond belief, too good to be true. The angel reminds them of the promise of Jesus, and confronts them with the empty tomb; his every word is a summons to believe. It is still a fact that there are many who feel that the promises of Christ are too good to be true. That hesitation can be dispelled only by taking him at his word.

(2) They are urged to *share*. When they themselves have discovered the fact of the risen Christ, their first duty is to proclaim it to and to share it with others. 'Go, tell!' is the first command which comes to all who have discovered the wonder of Jesus Christ for themselves.

(3) They are urged to *rejoice*. The word with which the risen Christ meets them is *Chairete*; that is the normal word of greeting; but its literal meaning is 'Rejoice!' Those who have met the risen Lord must live forever in the joy of his presence from which nothing can part them any more.

～

The doubter convinced

John 20:24–9

> But Thomas, who is called Didymus, one of the Twelve, was not with them when Jesus came. The other disciples told him: 'We have seen the Lord.' He said to them: 'Unless I see the print of the nails in his hands, and put my finger in the print of the nails, and unless I put my hand into his side, I will not believe.' Eight days later the disciples were again in the room, and Thomas was with them. When the doors were locked, Jesus came and stood in the midst of them, and said: 'Peace be to you.' Then he said to Thomas: 'Stretch out your finger here, and look at my hands; stretch out your hand and put it into my side; and show yourself not faithless but believing.' Thomas answered: 'My Lord and my God!' Jesus said to him: 'You have believed because you have seen me. Blessed are those who have not seen and who have believed.'

To Thomas, the cross was only what he had expected. When Jesus had proposed going to Bethany, after the news of Lazarus' illness had come, Thomas' reaction had been: 'Let us also go, that we may die with him' (John 11:16). Thomas never lacked courage, but he was the natural pessimist. There can never be any doubt that he loved Jesus. He loved him enough to be willing to go to Jerusalem and die with him when the other disciples were hesitant and afraid. What he had expected had happened, and when it came, for all that he had expected it, he was broken-hearted, so broken-hearted that he could not meet the eyes of others, but must be alone with his grief.

King George V used to say that one of his rules of life was: 'If I have to suffer, let me be like a well-bred animal, and let me go and suffer alone.' Thomas had to face his suffering and his sorrow alone. So it happened that, when Jesus came back again, Thomas was not there; and the news that he had come back seemed to him far too good to be true, and he refused to believe it. Belligerent in his pessimism, he said that he would never believe that Jesus had risen from the dead until he had seen and handled the print of the nails in his hands and thrust his hand into the wound the spear had made in Jesus' side. (There is no mention of any wound-print in Jesus' feet because in crucifixion the feet were usually not nailed, but only loosely bound to the cross.)

Another week elapsed and Jesus came back again; and this time Thomas was there. And Jesus knew Thomas' heart. He repeated Thomas' own words, and invited him to make the test that he had demanded. And Thomas' heart ran out in love and devotion, and all he could say was: 'My Lord and my God!' Jesus said to him: 'Thomas, you needed the eyes of sight to make you believe; but the days will come when people will see with the eye of faith and believe.' The character of Thomas stands out clearly before us.

(1) He made one mistake. He withdrew from the Christian fellowship. He sought loneliness rather than togetherness. And because he was not there with his fellow Christians, he missed the first coming of Jesus. We miss a great deal when we separate ourselves from the Christian fellowship and try to be alone. Things can happen to us within the fellowship of Christ's Church which will not happen when we are alone. When sorrow comes and sadness envelops us, we often tend to shut ourselves up and refuse to meet people. That is the very time when, in spite of our sorrow, we should seek the fellowship of Christ's people, for it is there that we are likeliest of all to meet him face to face.

(2) But Thomas had two great virtues. He absolutely refused to say that he understood what he did not understand, or that he believed what he did not believe. There is an uncompromising honesty about him. He would never still his doubts by pretending that they did not exist. He was not the kind of man who would rattle off a creed without understanding what it was all about. Thomas had to be sure – and he was quite right. In *In Memoriam*, Tennyson wrote:

> *There lives more faith in honest doubt,*
> *Believe me, than in half the creeds.*

There is more ultimate faith in people who insist on being sure than in those who glibly repeat things which they have never thought out, and which they may not really believe. It is doubt like that which in the end arrives at certainty.

(3) Thomas' other great virtue was that when he was sure, he went the whole way. 'My Lord and my God!' said he. There was no half-way house about Thomas. He was

not airing his doubts just for the sake of mental acrobatics; he doubted in order to become sure; and when he did, his surrender to certainty was complete. And when people fight their way through their doubts to the conviction that Jesus Christ is Lord, they have attained to a certainty that those who unthinkingly accept things can never reach.

❧

The kingdom and its witnesses

Acts 1:6–8

> *So when they had met together, they asked him: 'Lord, are you going to restore the kingdom of Israel at this time?' But he said to them: 'It is not yours to know the times and the seasons which the Father has appointed by his own authority. But when the Holy Spirit has come upon you, you will receive power; and you will be my witnesses both in Jerusalem and in all Judaea and in Samaria and to the furthest bounds of the earth.'*

THROUGHOUT his ministry, Jesus laboured under one great disadvantage. The centre of his message was *the kingdom* of God (Mark 1:14); but he meant one thing by the kingdom, and those who listened to him meant another.

The Jews were always vividly conscious of being God's chosen people. They took that to mean that they were destined for special privilege and for worldwide power. The whole course of their history proved that, humanly speaking, that could never be. Palestine was a little country not more than 120 miles long by 40 miles wide. It had its days of independence, but it had become subject in turn to the Babylonians, the Persians, the Greeks and the Romans. So the Jews began to look forward to a day when God would break directly into human history and establish that world sovereignty of which they dreamed. They thought of the kingdom in political terms.

How did Jesus see it? Let us look at the Lord's Prayer. In it, there are two petitions side by side. 'Your kingdom come; your will be done on earth as it is in heaven.' It is characteristic of Hebrew style, as any verse of the Psalms will show, to say things in two parallel forms, the second of which repeats or amplifies the first. That is what these two petitions do. The second is a definition of the first. Therefore, we see that, by *the kingdom*, Jesus meant a society upon earth where God's will would be as perfectly done as it is in heaven. Because of that, it would be a kingdom founded on love and not on power.

To achieve that, men and women needed the Holy Spirit. Twice already, Luke has talked about waiting for the coming of the Spirit. We are not to think that the Spirit came into existence at this point for the first time. It is quite possible for a power always to exist but for people to experience or take it at some given moment. For instance, no one invented atomic power. It always existed; but it was not until the middle of the twentieth century that anyone was able to access that power. So God is eternally Father, Son and Holy Spirit; but there came a special time when people experienced to the full that power which had always been present.

The power of the Spirit was going to make them Christ's witnesses. That witness was to operate in an ever-extending series of concentric circles – first in Jerusalem, then throughout

Judaea; then Samaria, the semi-Jewish state, would be a kind of bridge leading out into the world beyond Israel; and finally this witness was to go out to the ends of the earth.

Let us note certain things about this Christian witness. First, a witness is someone who says: 'I know this is true.' In a court of law, hearsay is not accepted as evidence; witnesses must give an account of their own personal experiences. A witness does not say 'I think so', but 'I know.'

Second, the real witness is not of words but of deeds. When the journalist Sir Henry Morton Stanley had discovered David Livingstone in central Africa and had spent some time with him, he said: 'If I had been with him any longer, I would have been compelled to be a Christian – and he never spoke to me about it at all.' The witness of Livingstone's life was irresistible.

Third, in Greek, the word for *witness* and the word for *martyr* is the same (*martus*). A witness had to be ready to become a martyr. To be a witness means to be loyal whatever the cost.

The glory of departure and the glory of return
Acts 1:9–11

When he had said these things, while they were watching, he was taken up and a cloud received him and he passed from their sight. While they were gazing into heaven, as he went upon his way, behold, two men in white garments stood beside them; and they said to them: 'Men of Galilee, why are you standing looking up into heaven? This Jesus who has been taken up into

heaven from you will come again in the same way as you have
seen him go to heaven.'

THIS short passage leaves us face to face with two of the most difficult ideas in the New Testament.

First, it tells of the ascension. Only Luke tells this story; and he has already given an account of it in his gospel (Luke 24:50–3). For two reasons, the ascension was an absolute necessity. One was that there had to be a final moment when Jesus went back to the glory which was his. The forty days of the resurrection appearances had passed. Clearly, that was a time which was unique and could not go on forever. Equally clearly, the end to that period had to be definite. There would have been something quite wrong if the resurrection appearances had just simply petered out.

For the second reason, we must transport ourselves in imagination back to the time when this happened. Nowadays, we do not regard heaven as some place located beyond the sky; we regard it as a state of blessedness when we will be with God for all time. But in those days everyone, even the wisest, thought of the earth as flat and of heaven as a place above the sky. Therefore, if Jesus was to give his followers undeniable proof that he had returned to his glory, the ascension was absolutely necessary. But we must note this. When Luke tells of this in his gospel, he says: 'they ... returned to Jerusalem with great joy' (Luke 24:52). In spite of the ascension, or maybe because of it, the disciples were quite sure that Jesus had not gone from them but that he was with them forever.

Second, this passage brings us face to face with the second coming. We must remember two things about the second coming. First, to speculate when and how it will happen is both foolish and useless, as Jesus said that not even he knew the day and the hour when the Son of Man would come (Mark 13:32). There is something almost blasphemous in speculating about something which was hidden from even Christ himself. Second, the essential teaching of Christianity is that God has a plan for us and the world. We are bound to believe that history is not a haphazard conglomeration of chance events which are going nowhere. We are bound to believe that there is some divine far-off event to which the whole creation moves and that, when that final fulfilment comes, Jesus Christ will be Judge and Lord of all. The second coming is not a matter for speculation and for a curiosity that is quite out of place; it is a summons to make ourselves ready for that day when it comes.

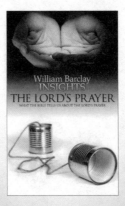

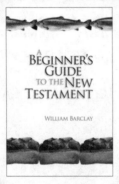